COLLECTED POEMS
Neil Tracy

Borealis Press
Ottawa, Canada
1975

ISN 0 919 594 395

Published with assistance of the
Canada Council

Cover Design by Le Phan

The Borealis Press Limited
9 Ashburn Drive
Ottawa, Canada, K2E 6N4

Printed and Bound in Canada

COLLECTED POEMS
NEIL TRACY

PREFACE

At the age of retirement some men feel the need to write their autobiographies, others simply collect their poems. This collection of Neil Tracy's poems is the record of a lifetime rich in observation and experience, the life of a man totally blind since his early twenties who has nevertheless seen more than most of us see and felt more than many of us feel.

The poems in this volume cover a wide range of ideas and emotions, sometimes basic and sometimes complex, but always the poems themselves are simple and direct. They express the reactions of a sensitive, honest man to the world around him and to the world within him. The twin twentieth-century curses of invasion of privacy and loneliness in a crowd are dramatized in poems such as "Variation on a Theme", "Going In" or "Camera Obscura". Neil Tracy can be bitter as in "Uncle Reuben" and "Social Service", but more often he is ironic or sympathetic. And occasionally he captures a single moment which swells into a whole realm of the human condition, such as in "At The Old Pithead" when the girl with the face of Saint Cecilia lifts her garment and calls out, "Hé, vieil Eddy, garde-moé", or when we catch a glimpse of "A silver beauty through a suburban window".

Neil Tracy does not fit conveniently into any school of poetry. He can be completely contemporary in content and form, speculating on pollution or Vietnam, but he can also write ballads and sonnets and recreate a few moments with Ben Jonson or Samuel Pepys. He can be equally humorous and serious, subjective and objective. But throughout he has a way with language, usually drawing from the commonplace to shape arresting images such as "You sewed the buttons on my life again" or "I'll drain my glass and climb the wooden hill".

Together the poems in this book move from the present and here to the past and distant, then back again. At the same time they move from the particular to the general then back to the particular. They speak of events, of people, of objects, of love, of pain, of joy, and of the courage to live fully and exult in the gift of life.

Ronald Sutherland

CONTENTS

8

VISION

Blind man, what do you see?
Blind men see ghosts.
They stand in the marketplace
To sell dead leaves for sand dollars,
Dead words and worn-out shifts,
Dead letters, dingy words like empty jam pots,
Rusty tunes on tin wire and plastic gut,
The last crumbs from the heavenly feast,
Rags from the veil of the temple.

VARIATION ON A THEME

How is it, love, we never are alone?
That man again — he's looking for his pay,
Concerned young saints to show the Jesus way,
The ultra-capable to fix the phone,
And then that virgin soul — the pregnant one —
She'd like to sign us up for *Sport And Play*
To help her on through night school come what may,
Two cats for milk, a dog about a bone.
How we would like some small time of our own!
A chance to prove each other, parts to play.
You just might do Zerlina to my Don,
Your innocence is charming, studied, gay;
You sing soprano, I lush baritone.
Non son più forte!
For another day.

WHAT'S NEW

Since we last met, what's happened? Let me see.
The joiner's hammer thudded in my ears,
Something broke down, there's talk of shafts and gears,
I don't much understand. It's time maybe.
The compact, too, to be or not to be.
The tailor's ripped his breeches with his shears,
The paradox has perished through the years,
What paradox? Why, one and one make three.

What is the use of squills and sleeping pills
Since every time you go you wet your feet?
What is the worth of lambs and daffodils,
While shibboleths and shillings still are sweet?
Perhaps I'll find a sibyl on the hills,
Or look for transmutations where we meet.

THE CITY

The city,
With no lore, no pity —
I was born here.

Ten cents for a glass of beer,
Ten cents for potato chips,
A dollar for a girl's hawn and hips,
So much for sweater and slacks.
Judgement comes in battery packs,
Wisdom from privy, church and floorshow.
I trip and bruise my brow.

I call for daisies and everlastings,
Clover lovely of dung and whitened bones,
Sermons wrested from stones,
Epitaphs cut by illiterate men,
Legends eroded by rain and the years,
Sweat carried under the sod by some
With their lies, their psalms,
And the seed of their casting,
And the not sparing of the rod.

LA ROSE AUX BOIS

The endless roar of traffic, stink and brawl,
The clink of coins, the gutters brimmed with rain,
The wise bad children squabbling in the lane,
Shrewd bastards of the sun in Montreal.
In squalid room with Christ upon the wall
She sleeps all day, then prowls La Place and Main,
With no more pleasure, no more pride and pain,
For men and men a dollar on the call,
And gets a whiff of sage at Bonesecours.
She's back downriver on a summer day —
The fish boats lying ready with their oars,
Staw hats, blue aprons moving through the hay,
The clean brown boys who whistle at their chores,
The shrine and bleeding heart beside the way.

NON NOBIS

The rest is silence where the day has done
With broken bottles, sticky dented cans,
With whizzing wheel, with stresses, struts and spans,
With wills and bills, with rag and hank and bone;
The miser's pittance which cannot atone
The curses, crosses, cads and Calibans,
The handful of small kernels which is man's
And just divides the Other from the One.

This is your fee from life, your bread and cheese,
A pot of porter at the evening's height,
A wayward kiss beside the willow trees,
A dwelling place you hold by squatter's right;
The windy wasteland where the senses freeze.
The rest is silence and the empty night.

BLINDNESS

I move in a state where they swing
Their knives wildly in the dark.
The girls hold their bellies in their hands
Like melons,
And probe my chastity not with their eyes,
But with words.

VETS IN SUBURBIA

These are the souls who spoke but yesterday,
Star-taunted keepers of the peace, lean men,
Knights of the ledger and the ballpoint pen
Whose sights are skylines, suburbs, pay.
Men who read papers on their homeward way
In bus and train, who keep the children when
The wife goes bowling; bed-at-ten
Dry gin and bitters, chapel-chorus clay.

They need not speak again, the day gone down
In red confusion past the smoking town.
Dumbly they stood and watched the gutted beast
Trailing his bloody tendrils to the east,
Some of them... Well, the grass is pretty high,
The sprinkler leaks, the pansy plants are dry.

DRAFTEE FOR VIET NAM

How shall I lie with you when I am dead?
Here, there's no sound but streams,
No stir but air teasing the pines,
No bonds but lips and hair,
No charge but these scant hours that shone and fled,
And so few words, so few stanch words were said,
No law but naked bodies strong and fair,
No pride, no price, no penitence, no prayer,
And still the dry thought rattles in my head,
Behind dumb doors the Five-Stars say their say.
The yellow bodies bend beneath the rod.
Our golden seed goes forth to mark the day,
And blood of our begetting stains the sod.
Down through the rice, the war-cart churns its way
And flings its refuse in the face of God.

CUSTODY

When you had gone
The silence was that of a sleeping tiger.
Dawn broke, a block of stone,
Showing the black and white of its grain.
A thought of our child came suddenly
Like a slap across the mouth.
The face on the pillow was that of a sad Sibyl,
Plastic white and endlessly wise,
With the dark salt of dead tears.
The half-blown breasts of twelve half-bared,
The little gold heart you once gave her
Trodden to glittering dust on the floor,
The big white bear of her cradle clasped in her arms,
Pressed hard against her body.
The silence was that of a sleeping tiger.
How was it that we did not hear?

UNCLE REUBEN

His fat ass grumbles on the softest seat,
Someone's tobacco clogs his pipe with tar,
When drinkers clink their quarters on the bar
His pot's as empty as a heifer's teat.
He must be careful what he gets to eat,
A blind man's pension don't go very far,
And where he lives, the nuns are so damn near,
You scarcely ever see a scrap of meat.
You who have eyes to see and hearts to hear,
He wrings the change from you, he haunts your door.
He has no eyes, the more he has your ear,
He spells the dark which all good men abhor.
Free meals, free whores, free 'baccy and free beer —
Slick operator, who could ask for more?

SOCIAL SERVICE

Christ! Could I but be free of cash and kind,
Of heart and head, of blood and sweat and tears,
Fool letters from the fool I never met,
Tear-spilling vessel full of grace and wind;
This antic rout, the weird, the dumb, the blind,
Pert unwed mothers with their waists high set,
Misgotten infants with their pants well wet,
All wheezing whining whooping human kind.
Rinsed from the stews and gin pots of the years,
Sprouts of the virgin capsule neatly cracked,
The living cuspidors for all our tears,
You come to me snot-nosed and flatus-packed,
Rank in assurance, stinking in your fears.
Oh, Godlike consummation of the act.

LE BON DIEU

He was probably twelve, and his beauty
And his rags were a classical thing.
He asked for a dime, "pour le bon Dieu",
While his eyes were as clear as a spring.
On his tongue was the guile of the serpent,
He wasn't one for idle regrets —
If there's one thing I hate it's a cynic.
Does le bon Dieu enjoy cigarettes?

SALVATION ARMY

A hymn flings up the evening like a blind,
The drums and trumpets marching as to war,
The cross of Jesus going on before,
Three Christian soldiers weaving on behind.
So that which should have been a shroud shall bind
The wounds of someone stricken by the door,
And loaves and fishes feed the crowd once more,
One piece in thirty mends a broken mind.

This is your term: to set a spirit free,
An aching hungry belly must be fed.
The wine and wafer of the Pharisee
Transmutes to coffee and a crust of bread.
That red merino with the appliqué,
My dear, I met it in the Street today.

PARABLE

I saw her
Sitting among the tares in her red sack
Thinking upon the bad seed.
Someone told her the parable
Of the five loafers and the two fishers,
But she said she knew all about that.
While she sat brooding,
And while the swineherds rushed down the hill
Into the sea,
His friends burned the carpenter's shop
To the ground.

CECILIA

There is the smell of angels in this place,
Where toast and tea beget a miracle,
Where saints and seers bestride the carousel
That half-baked thought and half-dead music pace.
"I'm blind", she murmurs, from her state of grace.
The small hands pick, the great dead eyes repel,
"My heart fails not, although I walk in hell,
For I shall see my Saviour face to face."
And I am sick, for this sick want of sin
As putrid as dead flowers on the air.
God, where does sweetness end and rot begin,
Where septic and aseptic share and share?
And I think, Christ O for an ounce of gin
To take away this venom of despair.

21

AT THE OLD PITHEAD

In this place the sun is darkness and the moon will be blood.
Small evil things leap squirm and crawl in the hot dust,
Heat throbs like a pump and heaves up spurts of dry stink,
The saurian frame of the dead cable trails along the scarred fault,
Time surveys Armageddon through the skull of the dead derrick.
On the rim some crazy houses, sagging and gaunt
Like old women of much bearing, lean ear to ear.
A few children with death mask faces, peer, poke and scratch
And relieve themselves as the slow spirit moves.
A young girl, with the face of Saint Cecilia,
Lifts her one garment to her navel and cries,
"Hé, vieil Eddy, garde-moé."

ANTHRAX

Asaph the calf hung to his mother's spurting dugs.
The knacker quibbled, his silver in his hand,
His mallet behind his back.
Asaph was worth only his liver, his hide and his heels,
But Miss Muffet must have her curds and whey,
Goldilocks, her porridge and her cream;
Glue is needed to hold Good News together,
Calfskin is used to bind up psalms.
Anemic old men require calves' liver
To keep the vitals from turning blue.
So a bargain was struck, and the knacker knocked.
But the knacker pricked his thumb and died.
His hide, his heels and his liver
Were not worth his damnation.

1867

Grim tales behind dumb doors! The soft-soap smell,
Scarlet geraniums behind starched lace.
There is no shadow on the ivory face,
Talk of the square white chapel and its bell.
Who would believe her youth had passed in hell?
An iron father of a crooked grace,
A calf-bound mother of Sapphira's race,
Who dared not look into each other's well.
Pa and Ma lie beside the graveyard gate,
As though they loved, at least the writing says.
Incest asleep, also the living hate,
Save in the faded peepshow of old days.
Behind the blooms and lace the pale eyes wait,
And wondering watch the folly of men's ways.

LET US NOW PRAISE

Down from the stead to where the river shrills
Spread checkered fields of young oats and old hay,
The town a psalm in white and granite grey
Shielded by elms and bucklered by the hills.
Within, they strove with God and codicils,
And got no children on the Sabbath day.
And when the word was said, they went their way
Palled in black broadcloth, flounces, hoops and frills.

The word of God was meat for stern debate
Set forth with rich brown splatter from the plug.
Wives and increase were part of man's estate
With chamber, moustache-cup and shaving mug.
Prim texts in worsted, morals on a slate,
Clandestine sport and smuggled whisky jug.

CRANBERRIES

Hers was the beauty
And wisdom of the psalms,
The anger of the prophets,
The lore of lye soap and buckwheat.
She went to meeting in a hat
Much like one of her saucepans.
Her hopes were fixed
Where Eden's bowers bloom,
But she watered the cabbages.
When her day's work was done
And she lay down beside her poor old man,
She knew that God was not dead.

ELEGY IN A COUNTRY GRAVEYARD
(Obiit 1823)

Abraham and Abigail
Span the wool and swang the flail,
Read the Word and wound the horn,
And got their brats on husks of corn.
Of eleven of his leaven,
Seven passed from womb to heaven
Followed by their mother's tears.
Their good father through the years
Ever cheers and perseveres,
Sternly strives to copulate
This new land to populate.
Let us then though ills beset us
Praise the sires that did beget us.

WITNESS AT THE DOOR

Hail Comely and Clean,
You have been washed in the waters,
Fanned by the spirit,
Your hair smells of dead flowers.

You saw the dove descend,
They say you tasted all wisdom.
Why hasn't it taught you to be kind?
Why haven't you got a single idea?

I haven't been blessed like you,
But I put out my hand to all men.
How come you're the only one
Going to get to heaven?

REVIVAL

The hymns shatter
The calm of the crystal sea.
Prayers and coffee beans rattle
On the canopy like hail.
They bathe you in blood,
They give you a pass
And credit card.
They are all very happy,
They have made God laugh.

NURSERY RHYME

The moon's a crooked sixpence in the sky,
The tailor's coat's too warm — he's dead in hell.
A groat's worth of regret, it's duff to pie
He doesn't know the farmer's in the dell.

Who knows who lays the linen to her loins?
She sings the tinker's song, he died in wrath.
She dances for a clutch of tarnished coins;
See how the cook pours hemlock in the broth.

What if the frolics and the fiddles rake
Old jagged tunes out of a ragged book?
We'll dream on devil's food and wedding cake,
And fry on Moll's or on the devil's hook.

This love's a hearty beast, a unicorn,
A mess of dotage with a crumpled horn.

RETRIBUTION

The Night, a tattered beggar old and bent,
Plodded along beneath a heavy load,
While we in fury lay beside the road
And fell on him and robbed him as he went.

He knew our bondage, how we often met
Abroad to give our hooded spirits scope,
Yet like a spy came creeping back to grope
With shaking shining fingers in the wheat.

He cried and flung his sack from him in flight,
Which we straight ravished, kneeling on the earth,
Such things as beggars prize, of little worth
Grey rags of cloud and tinkling chips of light...

Then fear beset us, and we fled the place
Lest day should take us in so mean a case.

MUTATION

You gave me a cup of water
And a crust of bread, my friend.
But we ate what we ate with laughter
And dreamed no dreams at the end.

Now we look at each other coldly
Over dishes of cunning shapes,
And the cake that we eat is mouldy
And our wine is from sour grapes.

ST. PIERRE, ILE D'ORLÉANS

O, the bells around the island, they ring at six o'clock,
When he's coming in to breakfast from the feeding of the stock,
And he leans upon the half door and he says a little prayer,
With the gentle wind from Gaspé pulling at his silver hair.

O, the bells around the island, they ring at six o'clock,
When he's coming from the meadows from the tying of the shock,
And he leans upon the hurdle and he says a little prayer,
While the wind of many sunsets tugs his wisp of silver hair.

SONG ON A MAY MORNING

The cock's about it,
And nothing loath to shout about it.
Two blackbirds rattle in a battle,
Poor Renard is already a dupe, if only he knew it.

The violets and wet-the-beds kneel on their shins,
Thinking of yesterday's sins.

Molly sings of flute and goat,
Mending the rent in her petticoat.
Brown boys swell with hope,
Girls cope.

O, beshrew it, beshrew it!
Get lost in the fog,
You old dog!

BALLAD OF BOY BLUE

Find me a beautiful corner to sleep
I am so weary of tending the sheep,
Lulling the lambs with a Bergamasque air
Played on a flageolet, somber and deep,
Tying their ribands and combing their hair,
Getting them ready for Widdicombe Faire.
Buy me a halter-rope, buy me it cheap,
Find me a beautiful corner to sleep.

I am so tired of counting the sheep,
Hunting the strays on the crest of the steep,
League upon league through the rain and the cold,
Bringing them tenderly back to the fold.
But Life leads the band with a much wider sweep.
The goats on the mountain have silver and gold,
So under the fold-fence they wriggle and creep.
Find me a charming small corner to sleep.

Down where the brown-handed gleaners do reap,
I met Miss Muffet and Little Bo-Peep,
I kissed them both beside Dalliance Well,
They told the parson and he tolled the bell.
With bell book and candle all piled in a heap,
He sent me a-packing and howling to hell;
Then for his trouble he drove off my sheep.
Find me a quiet cool corner to sleep.

L'envoi

O fool, you have excellent reason to weep,
You bartered your wares to a Kiss-and-Go-Tell,
So put on your motley and jangle your bell,
And find you a lonesome sad corner to sleep.

LOW MASS

Drear March morning rain obdurate
Frowzy server drowsy curate
Gospel drone Epistle mumble
Wheeze and sneeze and belly grumble
Aching knees and buttocks quaking
Paschal parish breakfast making
Child in corner smacking toffee
Dear God turn my thoughts from coffee.

CONCLUSION

The weirds and wizards wheeze and whine,
The fringes finagle and opine.
I gaze into my glass of wine
And watch the living rubies shine.
I contemplate the feuds and flashes,
The doctors' hoods and canons' sashes.
I count the diamonds on her lashes,
And hold all else is dust and ashes.

MARY CAME DOWN FROM THE HILLS

Mary came down from the hills
To walk for a while by the sea,
She carried a cluster of bittersweet
Which she crumpled and gave to me.

She had bathed in the icy water
Which springs from the rock and the snow,
For she was the snow's chaste daughter
Where only white flowers grow.

When she went back to her high white waste
She bore on her hand which was white and chaste
The stain of poppies she'd picked by the sea.
But the stinging touch and the herbal taste
Stayed long with me.

BOREDOM

Twenty little golden spoons
Stirring flimsy cups of coffee,
Ten exquisite macaroons,
Talk like vinegar and toffee.

Twenty little golden forks
Primly tease the tender waffle,
And the popping of the corks
Says they think most things are awful.

Ten narcissi, fags in holders,
With attendant many clippers,
Lean upon each other's shoulders,
Ogling one another's zippers.

Cornered thus by Claude and Basil,
And a desiccated chippy,
Woolly palate, lazy nasal,
God I wish I were a hippie!

FIDDLE TUNE

Woodpecker pecking on the graveyard pine,
Night wind rattling the doors and sashes,
Up there talk about their bread and wine,
Down here nothing but dust and ashes.

Over the road lives Deacon Nye,
Owns nine daughters and a throne on high,
And here I am with Imogene,
Only her virtue and a hope between.

Barn owl sitting on the warped ridgepole,
Blinking his eye at our rock and shoal,
Mad fiddle screeching out the do-si-do,
Lodestar winking though red calico.

Bedbug clicking through the cornhusk ticking,
She and me are pretty poor picking,
For we've been sent to Poverty Peak
To a shack and a stove and meal for a week.

Grey mouse gnawing on the corner log,
You'd do much better on the preacher's hog,
Nothing for the baby but pork and grits,
His ma's got consumption, and he's got fits.

Black crow tugging at the meeting house bell,
Soft soap slicking up the road to hell,
A psalm and a shove and a one, two, three,
Down goes baby, mother and me.

Black rat slinking though the crazy stones,
There ain't much meat on these here bones,
Black rat chipping at the coffin lid,
There's something here that's better hid.

AS YOU LIKE IT

Let Mozart charm me
Haydn disarm me
Wagner quiver me
Verdi shiver me.
But by shock or scandal
By bell book and candle
The good God deliver me
From terrible Bach and horrible Handel.
I tend to choke
On anything baroque.

HAIR UNDER THE FLOOR

I am long dead,
The bones of those I love are scattered among the stones,
Their dust at this time falls on Palmyra.
I hold in my claw the tooth of a hound,
The women come to their doors
To pour out the water from their lentils,
Men drain the dregs from their cups
And knock out their pipes against the hubs of carts.
Lovers come at night
And I hear on the dry ground the thud of their crises.
Here is a little gold charm
Fallen from the wrist of a great beauty;
It shows Venus and Ceres
Bound together by a chain of little adders' heads.
Here is a desert seed
Which will snap like a Chinese squib
At the touch of a drop of water.
Death still hangs on life
Hair under the floor of an old barbershop.

MADONNA

This crude clay figure lies in my palm
Like the handle of a tool.
With her bent back, her deathless Giotto face,
Her squill-headed infant resting along her arm,
As grained as rough-cast
Chipped around the edges,
Stained duly blue with the blood of some common weed,
Shaped by some hard hand,
Soiled with earth and sweat,
Who knows where or when,
Yet deep in the charm of all small harmless things.
Sacrum and amulet of the dairy barn and corncrib,
Clasped to the womb of some scared innocent,
In the dark night of her trouble and triumph.
Daughter of shepherds,
Wife to the carpenter,
Earth-mother,
Mistress of heaven,
Give back to us your ancient wisdom
Sacramental toil love and sleep
Wheatcakes and milk.

DEAN PRIOR

I dream and sometimes fancy I could go
To that Proud Parish rich in daffodil
To pass one Devon twilight still and slow
And sense the sea not far beyond the hill.
That old grey priest, young England's sweetest voice,
To lean beside me on the gate a while,
Tracy to heel, pipes fuming, ale to choice,
Lend me his fertile eye, his tricksy smile.
Ben's in the Abbey standing in his grave,
I exiled here, glad Cheapside far away.
Then the earth turned and nights and days were brave,
New spring, green gowns, the taunting pipes of May.
Lighten our darkness, Friend, improve our rhyme,
Beyond this waste of seas, this wall of time.

THE CAVALIER

I took my child into my arms and kissed her.
I put her dowry into her hand
And placed her in the arms of her lover —
They never looked up.
I took my young mistress into my arms
And kissed her asleep.
I looked into my purse —
There were three gold coins left;
I gave one to my bastard,
One to the priest,
And one to my old servant,
And told them to go.
I heaped the fire high with cedar,
I took the crucifix from the wall
And flung it into the flames.
I turned the king's picture to the wall.
I broke my sword across my knee.
I sought my old brother
Where he lay bemused upon his bed
And killed him with my dagger.
I looked to the table with its bottle of red wine
And loaf of white bread.
And now I go to the door,
Where the gentle stranger has waited long.

MOZART

I spied you sporting by the linden trees,
And she so young in frosty virgin blue,
Pouting while you went scouting for her shoe,
Your powder smeared, and grass stains on your knees,
Giovanni and Zerlina, if you please!
It's God's good summer, so the May wine's new.
You kissed the Empress once, La Marquise too.
There's nothing in the safe but bread and cheese,
There's time to fret, old Sigismund's a fart;
The boys need breeches, put Christ's peace on them.
Constanze is big again — that rocks the cart.
Dress and redress gone frayed along the hem,
Slim harvest shadows etch a summer art,
Death counts his change and buys a requiem.

LAZARUS

I am sitting under the table of Dives,
I can just see his hand on the knee of an idol.
His greyhounds are compassionate
But I avoid their morbid curiosity.
He knows I am here
And lets fall a mince pie.
Maybe he remembers that I once gave him a crust of bread
And a cup of water.
They say that I am to lie in the bosom of Abraham,
But that is small comfort.
He may also make paradise
Through the eye of a needle.

ELECTRA

A fresh pie bubbles on the window-sill,
A ginger cat naps in the rocking chair,
The black stove roars, its mica eyes aglare,
The tang of soap, sage, vinegar and dill.
Yet here the air is cold and very still;
You mind the fettered Samson overstair,
The hungry wife caught in a vicious snare,
The white-faced girl, her dark eyes fierce to kill.

The world of plow and yield is blotted out.
In that vague limbo void of sight and sound.
He yearns to touch her as she moves about,
Her frigid deftness holds excess in pound.
And so he aches with agony and doubt;
His own old treasons pin him to the ground.

SACK

I see the low dark bodega with its rows of barrels.
You expect a bony head glowing with mould
To pop out of each barrel, as in Saint Calixtus.
The doomed little mice squeak and scuttle after the dry crusts.
Diego, not he of Compostela, with his guitar, sings of the Moors.
At the little tavern the drink is as dry as sarcasm on the tongue.
We break the crisp crust on the brown earthen dish;
The coiled baby cuttlefish beneath is a silent shock.
Old fat Sir John gulps and belches.
Burly Ben roars with rage, flings his cup on the table,
And lets fly a great fart.
Will grins in his blond beard
Showing the sweet, red bow of his lips
And swears by the heels of the Duke of Clarence.
Sam Pepys washes down a monstrous oyster and tells
Of how his mother passed a kidney stone in the coal hod.
Under the willows by the Cam, the old dons sip and drone,
Casting out pearls and fossils.
John sits in the arbour,
Bantering with the five fair daughters of Domecq,
With the two fond fathers looking on.
One says, "Shall we marry him to Delia?"
Pedro smiles sadly and shakes his head.

APRIL 23rd, 1564

God how this wind bursts from the guts of night!
It crams the bellman's croak back in his teeth
Who with his bell his brown bill and his light
Catnips his way to Clopton's bridge beneath.
The mad wind hisses into good men's dreams
And tortured trees cast horrors on the glass.
Up in the chamber, Mary Arden screams,
The midwife curses, spits, and rakes her ass.
The wind blew Master Slender's chimney down,
It tossed the lenten fare off Yarmouth town,
It shook the sleepers under Elsinore,
But dawn brought April's kindlier eye once more;
Fair florins jingled in the midwife's purse,
Dame Mary set her infant son to nurse.

CANZONE

The dapper dandy with the trim black beard
Wrought out his winning lines to suit his tune,
Of pope, duke, minstrel, painter or buffoon,
The hawk on wrist, the black boar newly speared,
Brown girls among the grapes their lips red-smeared,
Laura's green eyes, Giulia beneath the moon,
A furtive love that broke and passed too soon,
The white hand kissed, the tall lad gloved and geared.
So neatly caught and crystalled in his hand,
The fluid hours of duke, clerk renegade.
He knew the tale was written in the sand,
Who held the counter when the throw was made,
That love and death forever cronies stand,
And wine and wormwood on men's lips are laid.

BLACK DEATH

The chantry priest of Cock Lane preached a parable
To a drab
And to a system of human bones
Sitting thigh to thigh on a dead sailor's seachest
Their bare feet in the straw.
Lice ticked in the straw.
Nobody knew
There was a gold coin
Lost in the straw
And a little bag of silver in the chest.
They all went to bed hungry.

44

BIOGRAPHICAL NOTES

I

He sipped his wine
Smoked his pipe
Flogged his pupils
And justified God's ways to man.
He lost his way
In a cloud of auburn hair.
He stood,
Mary waited.

II

His bones lie in Bunhill
Between the tiger and the lamb
Where they laid him.
But I just saw him on the Barbican
Painting old Milton's portrait
With a treeful of angels
Watching in at the window
Over God's shoulder.

St. Olave's bell — night comes and you are gone,
Rain patters on the plane leaves in the yard,
Off in the house I hear poor Deb cry hard.
I lock the door, and so to bed alone.
I lie in sweat and gnaw a shrewd old bone;
The whores beset me, many a clownish word,
A cuff or two maybe; forgive me Lord,
Till candles gutter tears upon the stone.

These devil's candles bring the place to life.
There's quality below, set haunch to hook,
Put out the sack, tune virginals and fife,
Tickle the jacks, turn out the ballad book.
Lay out the saffron petticoat, pert wife,
Be quick my linnet; eh, you wenching rook.

CANTICLE

She has slept for ages in the shade of great leaves.
Nothing rouses her save the sound of one voice,
Whereupon she stirs and sighs.
Why then does Anacreon sing?
The young men beat on the table with their books,
The girls come with blood on their bare white feet?
What means the fall in the orchard of the pears and apricots,
The wild tumult of red and white flowers,
The fornication of candles with the night wind?
There is a beggar in the street under the rain;
He has a patch on one eye, a fiddle with one string and a bird
in a cage.
He feeds his bird on worms he digs from the black mould of the
swamp;
They are rich red worms, fat on the ashes of dead orchids.
The bird sings because his crop is full,
The man sings because his belly is empty.
His is the only voice that she hears.
Why then does Anacreon sing?

SEA IDYL

He sits in his cabin, throned on his chest of doubloons
Jewelled with barnacles.
His West Indian mistress sits at his feet, her nakedness
No longer a reproach.
There is a bronze dagger at her feet,
On the floor twinkle the bits of a broken rosary,
Eels slide by like streaks of light,
Flinty cancers speed over the milky ooze on horrendous legs.
Long shadows as pulled by strings pass steady and slow,
And little dragons in castles draw in their heads.
Strange bright flowers rise and spread
And move with the ebb and flow.
Where are the pheasants and wine, the plackets and codpieces,
The passepieds, and pavanes,
The fine books on old brown vellum, the songs,
The poems and the prayers?
All that die must go down to the sea.

ADAGIO

As through dim chambers of the past I move,
A house alive with echoes and quick shade,
A web of broken tunes and old charades,
Touched with the scent of dusty rose and clove,
I pause to dally with an ancient love
Foregetful that those clean white limbs are made
One with the shattered glass and mouldy spade,
The wine once spilled, the compact yet to prove.

And my life cries, Let not one novice die,
Let Beauty wrest her tribute from the years
To dream through hair and kisses on the sky,
With harps and tambours thudding in her ears,
Oh, it is cold where dear young lovers lie
With faded blossoms wetted by our tears.

EDEN

I see the long green challenge of the hill
Crowned with old maples, lusty yet and stout,
The broken wall, where snakes slide in and out
To view our Fall with hooded eyes and chill.
Dead gods in motley walked there through the thrill
Of frosty evenings, casting tares about,
And bitter-hearted apples, fair without,
The fruit you proffered which I savour still.

One time I kissed and tears gleamed on her face,
The sickle fell between, and Eve was gone.
Then Lillith kissed and straight in that dark place
The hard hot apples of enchantment shone.
We closed until the seed of our embrace
Lay in her body like a witch's stone.

DAYBREAK

The old square window with its sixteen panes
Gave on a world of joy and pregnant chance,
Gemmed crags, weird woods, high skies, the lake's expanse,
Portages, whisky trails and haunted lanes.
I wake to find her mules beneath my chin.
Green mocking eyes, as flat of chest as I.
We romp in whispers not to wake The Spy,
Then sense that elsewhere there are worlds to win.
Some frank arrangements, we are in array.
The dog enlists with rusty yawn and shake.
The squeaking stair, disaster lies that way.
The kitchen won, milk, apples, johnnycake;
Then out into the wonder of the day,
To the serene blue optic of the lake.

HOME BEFORE CURFEW

The moon is a crinkled pink shell
Hung in the haze.
The day empties its last cup
Agains the wall of the church on the hill
And plays geometric games with the windows,
Garden hoses hiss
Spit up sparks like the snake of fables,
A cool breath moves along the ground
And bathes our bare legs,
Warm puffs tickle out noses with street smells
Pipe smoke and the common blooms of suburbia.

We pause in the cover of the lilacs for a quick kiss,
Both feeling that it is forbidden fruit.
Over her head I see the kid who carries the *Montreal Star*
Zigzagging down the street from porch to porch.
There is a cab in front of Miss Cox's house;
The cabman and the maid waft her to her door
One on each arm
She wailing for them not to rush her so.

There is a scuffle about the fare from the station,
The cabman leaps to his seat
Swearing softly in French.
Strange irony — the old horse breaks wind.

She jerks her hot cheek from my lips
And flies down the street on a froth of white intimacies.
Something tells me that it is best not to follow
But I linger in the shade of the lilacs.

Down in the freight yard
A little switcher puffs and frets
Snaking out cars of lime and pulpwood.
Across the street two neigbours rumble earnestly on a porch
The smoke from their pipes bellying out into the streetlamp.
Up in her room a light goes on
And a shade is drawn.

THE INLET

There is an inlet at the field's far end.
A White sand sparked with quartz bland to bare feet,
Trap for the sun, where earth and water meet,
A stand of spruce against the wind's rude tend;
A little golden Aphrodite lies
Naked along the ledge, and all things move,
Leaves, clouds and water; pudor, anger, love,
As wakes the ancient wisdom in her eyes.
And then life gave the third great sign to me,
Breathed on a hollow tube of fired clay;
I stood alone beside a boundless sea,
Face to the east against another day;
My back to that dark house of mystery
Where Mother, Daughter, Sister, Lover lay.

LITTLE GREEN SNAKE

My love caught a little green snake.
She coiled it round her wrist for a living jade
And wore it for a summer hour.
It was warm and content,
Then it left for its meal of drones
Dead for love at the feet of their queen
And little polished beetles.
Where the snake had been
There was a mark on her wrist,
A trace of blood.
I was angry and followed it
And killed it among the nettles and sour sorrel.
She was angry to tears,
So I walked away over the hills until I met a new day.

AFTERWARDS

She came to me in the dusk,
Her eyes wise and sad as sorrow.

What of tomorrow?
I have been with you from dark to dark,
From the cutting of bread to the drinking of warm milk,
From the crow of the cock to the dog's latest bark.
I have walked with you from the turning of sod
To the judgement of God,
From the sowing of corn, from the seed to the silk,
From the seed and weed to the sheaf and fallen leaf,
May to December.

Do you remember the willow mist, the locust musk,
The stink of dung on the grain under the rain,
Little snakes like green fire,
And the song of the stone on the scythe in the hay?

Do you remember the sun all day,
The reapers in straw to the loins,
The brown girls who sang to the flails
And cheese and cakes and cider in frothing pails,
And at evening the whispers,
The sighs and the clinking of coins?

Do you remember me,
The barefoot, the bearer of cups and plates,
The holder of bridles,
The swinger of gates?

AFTER DINNER

I watch and listen as the phrases race.
Dinner is done. Her mother playing Bach,
The music speeds, making a fugue with talk
Of boys, of books, of crudities in class.
And I think, stand and let the stages pass.
Gone the brusque kiss, child smell, the mucky smock,
The tattered books, the moppet's puppet walk.
From now on I shall see her through a glass.
A sharp woe smites; the old conspiracy
Becomes dim shapes, a worn transparency,
Halftones, bell notes, so like a pebble cast.
One flash of soul and beauty bright and fast
As when fresh from the bath, pert head aside,
Grinning and smart she flings her wrapper wide.

HAUNTED

Then she and I, the dog Sebastian,
Through a long summer rich in endless days,
Scattered our legend on a thousand ways,
And sowed our private harvest as we ran.
An untried Pan, and unscathed Circe sped
From grim Knox-haunted rooms to fantasy
Of fin fur feather flower lake and sky,
While the girl's taunting theorem ever fled.
When the old walls burned blue, the night storm swept
The black slates bright, and thunder charged the air,
And shuffling wheezing whispering
IT crept along the children's passage,
Down the stair; we clung in terror while Sebastian slept.
I sensed her rigid limbs and hot wet hair.

THE ATTIC

A rainy day — the murky bubbled pane
Pressed like a lid against the plum-black sky.
In this quaint midden of mortality,
We drooped, and scanned the whisper of the rain.
Decrepit chairs, whole charnels of maimed dolls,
A trunk of books as dead as Caesar's ghost,
Stiff in the mould of some departed host,
Stern sabbath trousers, black ancestral shawls.
The cool, sly breaths that titillate the nape,
The kisses of dead children, we were told.
The diligence of mice, the beetles' tap,
Glutinous webs on treasures Egypt-old
Kept wide eyes wandering from shape to shape.
She pressed me close, gave me her hand to hold.

COMPREHENSION

Your little boy eased beside me there
Was like the moon wrapped in two folds of mist.
The sombre eyes, the sleepy mouth I kissed,
The phantom sheen and shade on face and hair
Gave grace, but held decision in a snare,
So that long trains of dream enclosed our tryst
And life hung in a dark and silent cyst
Until one knocked and bade you forward fare.

I ever follow through a sleeping town
Past shuttered windows, muted fast-closed doors
To where a rough path leads unkindly down
To give at last upon time's slippery shores.
We'll find a key among the wreckage strewn,
A distant light, a boat with ready oars.

THE BATHERS

We lay together in the living light
And watched the currents build a shining ply,
And three grey peaks against a perfect sky,
Pizgah, Pope's Castle and The Widow's Mite.
Sebastian went belling though the brake
Coursing a whim. Where the dark mountains groined,
A sauntering sail. Sense and languor joined.
We lay and told the notions of the lake,
Glad with the dancing waves, the naughty air
That tickled our bare backs and tugged our hair.
For we were naked in the face of God,
With eyes unschooled, still spared of Aaron's rod,
Still uninfected by life's old slow wound,
Gold with the sun, barefoot on holy ground.

ON THE MOUNTAIN

Old Pea-eye took us on The Widow's Mite.
"You youngun's stay close handy, like she said,
You don't go up The Ledge or past The Head,
I got five cord to rassle now till night."
The dog raised spore and sped off on the chase.
We scrambled up the slope through slash and shale.
A tiny Colorado walled the trail.
Below, the old man's axing marked home base.
Teased Quasimodo shapes, knot-bludgeoned root,
Waif breaths, thin bastards of the shade and sun.
High on The Ledge from grizzled beard to boot
We saw Old Smallclothes leaning on his gun.
Dog went, a shadow from a witch's moot,
Then we too, down the gully on the run.

TWO MEN IN A SUGAR HOUSE

Tonight we sit and plot the moods of March.
The old oil lantern swinging on its beam,
The smack of folklore in the gluey steam,
Dry pine and maple belching in the arch.
Snow falls and whirls in draperies at it falls,
A mad wind yelps and rattles through the shakes.
The pine tops slashing like defensive snakes,
Our faces grill, backs chill against the walls.
In this vexed light he dozes, brow tipped back,
Old faun from ragged chin to tufted ear.
The day we raced the lightning to this shack
I nosed clean clothes, sweet sweat, her sodden hair,
Omens unproved, bits of a young girl's flak.
Oh, Jesus! Will she come again this year?

LETTERS

I see her on old mornings at the lake
When she lay with us needing to be changed,
Bemused by shapes that ranged and rearranged,
By cosmos of light, sound, motion just awake.
In a bright window reading on her knees,
An instant silhouette upon a rock,
Catching my toss a whirl of hair and frock,
Or candidly asleep beneath the trees.
The Jura looms across her letters home,
Small fretsaw houses on the quilted slopes,
Mary Shelley's creature, neat-muted hopes, tale of Groc,
The school caniche, her trip to Rome.
I see the vibrant presence of her room
And pen my answers in the summer gloom.

CLOSED CIRCUIT

Strange to see her in a long white dress,
A thin white ribbon in her shining hair,
Infirmaries of blooms that clog the air,
Our stately Granddam humbled by distress.
When night fell, bringing easement to the land,
And essence moved within the house, I came,
Knelt in the wavering light and breathed her name,
Closed the prized jackknife in the small brown hand.
Sometimes in autumn evenings, I surmise
Sebastian's busy patter as I go
Down to the old grey church where now she lies
Under grey stone, beneath the sun and snow.
Then while the brown leaves fall and grey goose flies,
I think what only she and I could know.

AND WHAT OF HER NOW?

And what of her now that the years have sped?
My hair is grey, I am well-versed in wine,
I am content, what has gone by is mine.
The songs have been well sung, the books well read,
The fire seems good on ancient shins widespread.
Dusk has been long with me, and autumn shine,
Life is a warm old robe where moods combine
With greens and browns shot with a splash of red.

It is to smile in fancy I have strayed
Behind the horns and drums of other springs,
When any vagrant kiss could give us wings,
And drums and horns the flowing rout conveyed.
Her image moves through all a blessed shade,
For she had been a world of lovely things.

DARK ASTERS

Sometimes I see dark asters in a vase,
Dull blossoms under amber glass.
She's gone old lad, she's off to Erehwon,
To domes and deltas to minarets and groves.
And you can't crash the gate where she has gone,
The key no longer fits, hot anger moves.
God damn it all, see what the years have done,
She'll never know how much the old man loved.

THE EMPTY HOUSE

I fragment scent and sight and echo here,
For life sticks to old walls like cooking grease.
Faint odours tickle as dim shadows tease,
Raw nerves repeat the creaking of a stair.
I test the essence on the heavy air.
Dry blood? Dead flowers? Birth, death and old disease,
And furtive sighs and sounds that trifle ease?
Sly shapes distress the eye and stir the hair.
I sit in penance on the dusty floor
And try to tap a source forever dry,
Empty of words, afraid to touch the sore
Here where a fair thing froze and mortified.
Then I go out and grimly shut the door
And fondly hope I close the past inside.

I.O.U.

You granted me a shrine where I may go
To meet the soul I loved before you came.
Strong winds blew down that idol long ago,
Potpourri strong with bittersweet, no blame.
For it was I who kissed her eyes asleep
And closed the small white fingers that contained
Life's ivory ebony in such a sweep.
Outside, the wind blew keenly and it rained.
How many times have hands and spirit met
Across the debts and credits of a life,
Hot anger flashed, dark moods then quick regret,
Humour and truth that shape a man and wife?
Hers are the golden fragments of a chain.
You sewed the buttons on my life again.

CYCLE

Your love lies on me like a cool white hand,
When I smell clover blown across the field
By the fresh breath of May. Or when the land,
Tired of the lusty sun and heavy yield,
Lies naked to the rain and tonic frost.
Or when the fox limps glumly through the wet,
Where the last nuts and apples drop. The ghost
Of that keen day, whispers and shadows yet,
Till snow and sun conspire to cheat the eyes
Into bright grains of ice along the lids,
And numb wood sings, and pain and passion rise.
And so the thin white flame burns slow and deep,
Until it sinks beneath the snow to sleep.

AT THE WINDOW

So much for sleep, one in a scarlet cap
Whistles five notes upon a silver shell,
Summer puts on bright tights that suit her well,
The elder throws gold nuggets in her lap.
Life moves on little shoes that tick and tap
And waits the summons of a distant bell,
Like children off to school. Sight sound and smell
Engendering, hold action in a trap.
The chime — and forth my shrouded senses fare
Across thin mists and solid rooftops where
Locked in its dream your tawny beauty lies
In troubled rapture under hooded eyes
To see the sun strip its crude drapes away
And watch you clothe it for this matchless day.

MALAISE

Tonight the snow sweeps in from frigid lands
Out of a bright eclipse below the sky
And builds a crazy etching for the eye
In black and white, of block, bar, twisted strands.
And so abroad into this night I go
To spy the sparrow quailing in the eaves.
November waxes, and disquiet weaves
A dark dilemma with the night and snow.
A haunting discord underlies our dreams,
Our calm love stirs and murmurs in its sleep,
As though through chink and keyhole bane creeps in
To needle at our ease with icy quills
Until the dawn in smoky orange streams,
A stinging smarting silence cold and deep.
And from the blood, red on the snow as sin,
The fox's trail leads far across the hills.

PENURY REVISITED

Through the long grass the pismires moved in hordes
A thin shape spun and slid beneath the steps.
I knocked — came rodent tumult on rough boards,
Red evil eyes winked from the burdocks' depths.
A small incursion like a foetal ghost
Stirred the starved leaves, made an uneasy sound.
From the sere sunflower on the ragged post
Hard scrawny seeds came rattling to the ground.
I knocked — a crusted nursing bottle rolled,
Leapt from the eaves and clattered to my feet.
My taut dread snapped, lashed back and went ice cold.
That odd faint puff of smell, corrupt and sweet!
I fled the ghost that always haunts that place,
With her great belly and her blotched pinched face.

CHRISTMAS DAY

Last night the wights forsook their sheep and goats,
And wizards hobbled camels to a star.
Tonight the crass militia ranges far,
Blood of innocents upon their coats.
The fishers weigh and haggle in their boats,
The bishops wave their staves and scheme and spar,
Bigots debate and heap up tow and tar,
Christian deplores, and slits his neighbours' throats.
And does He walk our hills and meadows green
Clutching our hopes, with tears upon His face?
And does He know that gift and grace have been
John Calvin's gift and Torquemada's grace?
His taste still rank with bitterness and spleen,
Two thousand sickly harvests in this place?

THE BROODING SEA

This brooding cosmos, cruel and serene,
Painter of pearl, blood coral, tinted shell,
Where ageless harvests ever ebb and swell
In dance of ruddy gold and copper green.
Here in this liquid twilight shapes are seen
To move in silver-grey like ghosts in hell,
And silence wavers to a distant bell,
Sperm and corruption link in slimy skein.
A timeless cosmos, little is sent back
Of thin white life lived in the dark alone,
A protein spring, now taut, now limply slack,
Coiled about wood all scored and hard as stone,
A puff of mist along the moon's bright track,
A plaintive note piped on a hollow bone.

ON SKATES

Lime fire,
Hard grey steel glint electric blue
Spin and reel on the screaming blade
At the point of her shoe.
This is the whine of the sprung band
The crack of the whiplash
The snicker of a blade
The split second
The cool hard plan well laid.
Yet
There are the breasts
The slim white thighs
And love in the dark eyes.

COOL TOMB

They are quiet down there
The lover and the loved,
Even with lip on lip and hair in hair
They are still and unmoved.

There is no sigh no quick whisper no breathing
Only beaded prayers in cold fingers,
No red roses for the brow's wreathing
Only the scent and the dream lingers.

So will it be for us when the Prince rises.
No more feast for the eye and the heart's lust,
Only a staying of council in the cool gloom,
Perhaps a wisp of thought which the wind surprises,
A little gold ring in the white dust,
And each keeping his state in the cool tomb.

FUNGOID

Skull-white, stink of the graveyard,
Shaped like a tainted phallus leprous and obscene,
Sickened I watched it rise.
Then madly, I beat it down with my cane,
As I would the head of a cobra.
It scattered in slabs,
Like stale pastry.
Hecate's tart stuffed with the germs of evil,
Shaped by crooked hands.

POLLUTION

When she fell asleep
I left her under a rowan tree
And came down from the mountain.
When I looked back
The mountain had disappeared in the mist.
The way I came
Was strewn with gnawed turkey bones
Broken bottles, bloody rags and dead flowers.
I turned out my pockets —
Silver enough for a pack of cigarettes,
Credit card, punch card for three meals,
Check for short beer.
I wonder how she sleeps under her rowan tree.

ROUT

Jacques Neupan plays his flute bestriding his chair
As a Hun his saddle,
One red eyebrow cocked, one red eye aglow
Like a hot coal,
His leering neck awry, a snowy waste of shirt with winking studs.
Do those slick black patents conceal cloven hoofs?
Notes gleam like icy glasses of white wine;
The music speeds like a pencil of white light
Over the faces of frantic children old with wisdom.
Little citron breasts, Parian bellies
With rose black navels, ivory thighs,
All whirling in a field of silence
Against old earth-brown boles glinting with resin.

CAMERA OBSCURA

In this subworld of silence and waif light
Morning and evening seem like yesterday.
Words crowd the mind but on the tongue's tip stay
As on the ear, heard silence of the night.
And the sole claim, her presence, warm and white,
And the slow click, like bone on fire-tried clay
That comes and goes and comes and turns away
In this odd world of sense and shapeless light.
Atonement has no price, consent no peace,
Hell has no torment, punishment no rod;
I live for words and tunes that have no cease,
Strong-scented flowers upon a wine-stained sod,
A long post-kiss to lie on at my ease,
The pagan ethos of a pagan God.

A CHANGE

Let me whistle my dog down on autumn wind,
The hill grass bowing before,
The swaying woods behind,
The clouds black-bellied silver-tailed slicking the sky.
Let me look into a child's eyes
To tell her of old singers.
Let me smoke my pipe
Savour my sack
Flavour my rest
Listen to my Bach
And not feel tired and strange, for a change.

DEEP AUTUMNAL

I am sad because it is November,
The leaves and the birds have gone.
In my mind are the dark ballads of Martinmas.
I think of eager boys and lusty girls,
Who now count pills and lean on canes.
Beauty is shapeless under wool and leather
Like turnips in a sack.
Friends skim through the dusk
Like ghosts without sound or substance.
The earth flaunts bare bones, no charity of snow.
There is no hell but hell
And rheum is its profit,
No consolation but dry sherry and oyster stew.

JANUARY — AND MAY

Look in the glass, old fool?
Isn't it time the mass began to cool?
Or did you see the loathing in her eyes?
Look in the glass, but hope not to be wise.

YOU MAY BLAME SIR THOMAS BROWNE

The wizard in the dirty green breechclout
His face mummy-dry
His eyes muddy gobs of futility
His beard like a fish's spine.
He digs into reality
With his hautbois piping to the vipers.

The seething pitcher with a dozen heads
Like tulip buds writhing
In the plant pot of Mithridates.
Lithe bodies striving for love
And freedom like golden houris,
The ceaseless hissing whisper
This is a prize fit for a queen
Then death like the clap of a bell.

THE WHITE CAT

She left. Vibration woke and spread its paws,
Thrilled, turned on itself and slept again.
Comfort was like a cat caught in the rain,
And every thought that passed showed its claws.
Her anger glittered into frigid fire
In bright green flints that burned like basic ice.
Her function was a triggered spring and vise,
The hot intention and the cold desire.
Isis unlimited, a snowwhite cat
Rose like a phantom to the gate's top rail,
Glanced with a green glass, then like a melting veil
Without a sound became a sublimate,
Till from the brake sprang up the twisted cry
Of love and hate that seemed to rip the sky.

MORNING

The sun rises, and flings out golden fertility from his chamber pot.
The puffins jet eastward in whole covens of flying nuns,
The breeze from the sea serves up cool thin slices of fish in aspic,
The sea clucks like an old hen scrabbling in the shingle.

Love, while you sleep I will toss my old lies out of the window
                                    into the sea —
The clock, my violin, a book, our bottle of wine.
They drop like dried inkpots, each leaving its stain behind.
There is no truth but bread and cheese, no wisdom but love,
So I will come back and lie beside you for a while.
Tonight the wind will blow sharp from the land
And bear us where that tortured tree points, out to sea.
Let us go naked and with empty hands, to be young again.

GOING IN

Day is bright afterthought behind a hill,
And all that is begged and bought
Is heaped on the night's stone sill.
The boy listened and caught
The voice of a bird, cool and remote,
Five notes on a forest flute.
But now the old man must go in,
While the hours chime, the sands run,
The clocks march, the stars spin.
The door shuts on the light and the song,
The night is long.
And when the hair, the eyes, the lips, the hands,
Are all gone.
We lie alone.

SUBURBAN WINDOW

Back through the door of that willow-pattern world,
Keyed by a daisy or a whiff of caraway,
Where we once stood in wonder, foot in air,
Twelve thousand grim and gaudy days gone by, I go.
Beneath a sky of stars that pricked the eye,
Speeding through air that burned the cheeks with frost,
Crystals glittered on her hair under the red cap.
A brusque kiss — we had our passage under a racing sky.
Beneath a green and singing willow
We were taken in tears, ashamed of our bodies,
But as innocent as the ice cream and lemonade.
I never saw her again until yesterday,
A silver beauty through a suburban window.

JUDGEMENT

And so the sea runs out; so far away
It murmurs on the very edge of sight,
And where the breakers tumble, picks of light
Flick back like sparks across the sands' dun-grey.
And so the day ebbs out, this blasting day
Whose active caustic severs nights from night
And leaves the lips and eyelids sore and tight,
And at our feet some shapes of ash and clay.

Hated and loved, you purpose to look back
To where the dead house smoulders in the plain.
I, loved and hated, to the windy track
Where the whipped sea flings up a fiery mane
With love and hate, with hands and lips burnt black,
In God's good time we're damned to build again.

OLD RED BLANKET

My uncle said, Your place is in the bank—
The chime of coin, the whiffle of the notes,
The cautious question, rates and bids and quotes
For dreary years, so my spirits sank.
One night I closed the vault and fled the place
To sniff the lilac under wider skies.
An old dog studied me with milky eyes,
And warmed to Indian summer for a space.
He tottered after me until the fall,
Then time outwore the senator and slave:
Sole relic of that sabbath and conclave,
I dug a pit our side the boundary wall,
And with our old red blanket for a pall
I left him there six paces from her grave.

AFTERTHOUGHT

Did you crave apples of your own to pick
Or hear the boar scream in the butcher's hand
Or throw out salt cake for the cows to lick
Or test the scent of sheep's dung on the land?
The hucksters deal out silver for the cream,
Fresh eggs by the basket, apples by the pack.
You had no time to nurse the living dream
Crammed in the bag you carried on your back.
The clack of leather on an iron earth,
A stray mouse busy in the coffee mill,
The cat's gone out, no cricket on the hearth,
My pipe is dead and time unwound stands still.
I'll drain my glass and climb the wooden hill.